Novel Thinking Lesson Guide

In Their Own Words

Abraham Lincoln

Novel Thinking Lesson Guides
Charlie and the Chocolate Factory
Charlotte's Web
Shiloh
In Their Own Words: Abraham Lincoln
George's Marvelous Medicine

Written by
Ryan P. Foley
Norman J. Larson

Graphic Design by
Annette Langenstein

Edited by
Patricia Gray
Kathy Erickson

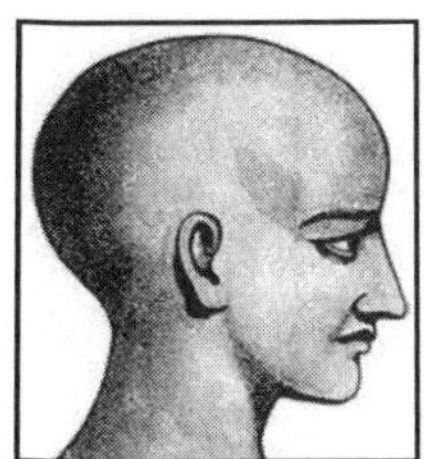

© 2009
THE CRITICAL THINKING CO.™
www.CriticalThinking.com
Phone: 800-458-4849 • Fax: 831-393-3277
P.O. Box 1610 • Seaside • CA 93955-1610
ISBN 978-1-60144-178-2

ABOUT THE AUTHORS

Ryan P. Foley received his BA in elementary education from Loras College. He has been a fourth-grade teacher since 2003. Mr. Foley has also taught special education students and has been a coach at summer camp.

Norman J. Larson received his BA in elementary education with a concentration in social studies from Clarke College. He has 15 post-graduate credit hours in the areas of literature and education. In 1999, he received National Board Certification as a Middle Childhood Generalist. He has been a teacher since 1994, and a fourth-grade teacher since 1996.

The authors wrote these lesson guides after trying unsuccessfully to find existing quality materials to teach novels effectively to students.

Table of Contents

Teaching Suggestions

The *Novel Thinking* books are student-oriented lesson guides, aimed at enhancing both reading comprehension skills and vocabulary. The intent is to provide structured, pragmatic, and easy-to-use supplemental classroom materials based on novels of interest to a particular grade level.

These lesson guides include the following language arts skills in the comprehension questions:

- Main Idea and Supporting Details
- Characters, Setting, and Plot
- Problem and Solution
- Cause and Effect
- Making Inferences and Predictions
- Drawing Conclusions
- Comparing and Contrasting
- Sequencing

The table of contents includes the skills used in each exercise.

Vocabulary skills such as context clues, synonyms, and naming parts of speech are emphasized. Writing activities that use descriptive writing are also included.

<u>Comprehension Exercises</u> Students are instructed to answer in complete sentences whenever possible.

<u>Scoring Methodology</u>

Comprehension

Each question has a possible total of 10 points.

- 5 points for content
- 5 points for grammar and punctuation

Students are awarded points based on the accuracy of their answers (content) and the format in which they provide the information (sentence structure).

All Other Sections

Each question is scored on content.

INFERENCES, FACTS, AND EVIDENCE

Inferences and Facts

In many of the activities in this book, you will be asked to draw a conclusion from information that is suggested in the passage. This is called *making an inference.* There is a difference between making an inference and identifying a fact. When you identify a fact, you are simply stating information that is given in the passage. When you make an inference, you are drawing a conclusion based on information that is not directly stated in the passage. In the following passage, see if you can tell the difference between an inference and a fact.

1. [1]The sun was shining; the birds were singing. [2]There wasn't a cloud in the sky as the bus went along. [3]It was going to be a beautiful day. [4]"A perfect spring day to be biking," thought Chai, as the bus brought him into the school parking lot.

   Fact: Birds were singing.
   Fact: It was a spring day.
   Inference: Chai is a student.
   Inference: Chai would rather be biking.

The facts are stated in the passage. The inferences require the reader to use information suggested by the story to draw a conclusion.

Examine the Evidence

When you make an inference about information from a story, look at the events described and the actions and words of the characters. Often an author uses the events and characters to lead you towards an inference he or she wants you to make. The events described and the characters' words and actions become evidence for your inferences. The more evidence you have to support your inference, the more likely your inference will be true. However, you must be careful when making inferences to identify and carefully examine your evidence. Otherwise, you may make an inference that turns out to be false. For instance, in the passage above, the author never directly says that Chai is a student who is riding to school in a school bus, but you can infer this. Your inference may be true. However, another possibility is that Chai is the bus driver. You need more evidence to determine who Chai is.

Read the next passage. What can you infer (or conclude) about Charlie's behavior?

2. [1]Charlie had taken my lunch box again and was holding it over his head. [2]"Come on, kid," he said. [3]"Try and get it." [4]We'd been through this before. [5]I knew it was no use trying to get it, but Charlie just loved to play this game. [6]As I grabbed for the box, Charlie tripped me, and I went sprawling on the concrete. [7]"Missed again, loser!" yelled Charlie, as he dumped the contents of my lunch box on top of me.

The passage doesn't state that Charlie is a bully. However, this conclusion is suggested by Charlie's actions. In sentence 1, Charlie takes the narrator's lunch box and won't give it back. In sentence 6, Charlie trips him as he tries to get his lunch box back. In sentence 7, Charlie dumps out the boy's lunch on his head. You can also infer that Charlie is a bully from his comments. In sentences 2 and 3, he teases the narrator. In sentence 7, he calls him a name.

Using Your Own Knowledge

Sometimes when you make an inference, you combine your own knowledge with the information that is suggested or given in the text. It is common knowledge that some snakes eat rodents. In the following passage, can you make an inference about what happened to the gerbils? Is there enough evidence to support your inference?

3. [1]Amanda was pet-sitting Alejandro's pet boa constrictor. [2]When she went to check on him in the morning, the snake was missing. [3]There also seemed to be fewer gerbils in the next cage.

It is possible that the snake and the gerbils escaped together. It is more likely that the snake escaped and ate the gerbils. It is a fact that boa constrictors eat small animals. Although the author doesn't give us this fact, we can use our own knowledge of boas to support this conclusion. In this case, our inference is probably true, but might be false. There is not enough evidence in the story to make a definite conclusion about the gerbils.

Name: ______________________________ **Date:** ______________________________

Pre-Reading Activity
K-W-L Chart
Abraham Lincoln

Directions for filling in the K-W-L chart:

1. Before reading the book, list any facts you know about Abraham Lincoln in the first column.
2. Before reading the book, list any facts you want to find out from reading the book in the second column.
3. After reading each chapter, list at least 1 fact that you learned from each chapter in the third column.

What I **Know** About Abe	What I **Want** to Find Out About Abe	What I **Learned** About Abe

What I **Know** About Abe	What I **Want** to Find Out About Abe	What I **Learned** About Abe

Name: ______________________ Date: ______________________

Chapter 1 "Introduction"

A. Vocabulary: Write the underlined vocabulary word next to its definition below. Then name the part of speech (noun, verb, adverb, or adjective) for each word.

1. "Four score and seven years ago, our fathers brought forth on this continent a new nation, **conceived** in **liberty** and dedicated to the **proposition** that all men are created equal."
2. At the time Lincoln gave the speech, the Civil War was **raging**.
3. Lincoln's **documents** (speeches and letters) are primary sources.
4. Lincoln felt that if the American nation were to split, it would be a severe blow to **democracy** everywhere.
5. In the final sentences of his Gettysburg Address, Lincoln sought to **communicate** this idea.
6. "... government of the people, by the people, for the people, shall not **perish** from the earth."

	WORD	PART OF SPEECH	DEFINITION
a.	____________	______	to be completely ruined or destroyed
b.	____________	______	happening in a strong and violent way
c.	____________	______	caused to begin
d.	____________	______	to make known
e.	____________	______	a form of government that is run by the people
f.	____________	______	freedom; independence
g.	____________	______	an idea or point of discussion
h.	____________	______	written communication

B. Synonyms: A synonym is a word that means the same or nearly the same as another. Circle the word that is a synonym to each vocabulary word.

Vocabulary Word	Choice 1	Choice 2
1. democracy	dictatorship	representation
2. raging	intense	calm
3. liberty	freedom	suppression
4. proposition	rejection	plan
5. conceived	created	destroyed
6. documents	speeches	papers
7. perish	die	live
8. communicate	report	silence

C. Comprehension: Answer the following questions in your own words using complete sentences. Use supporting details from the book where applicable.

1. What is the name of the important speech given by Abraham Lincoln during the Civil War?

   ___

   ___

2. Why was this speech important to the American people? Give 2 reasons.

   ___

   ___

   ___

   ___

3. How was Lincoln important to the history of America? Give 2 details.

   ___

   ___

   ___

   ___

4. To research Lincoln, primary and secondary sources were used.

Primary Source	**Secondary Source**
A document or physical object which was written or created during Lincoln's lifetime • Lincoln's Diary • A speech by Lincoln	Interprets and analyzes primary sources • A biography written about Lincoln twenty years ago • A history textbook written this year

Imagine you are going to write a report about your great-grandmother, who was a Navy nurse during World War II. Identify the following sources as primary or secondary that you could use to research information about the report.

__________________ a. a letter your great-grandmother wrote to her sister during the war

__________________ b. a picture of her taken when she was a little girl

__________________ c. a history book with a chapter on World War II

__________________ d. the diary your great-grandmother kept during the war

__________________ e. newspaper articles written years after the war

__________________ f. navy records from the war

Name: ______________________ Date: ______________________

Chapter 2 "Young Abe Lincoln"

A. Vocabulary: Write the underlined vocabulary word next to its definition below. Then name the part of speech (noun, verb, adverb, or adjective) for each word.

1. "If any personal description of me is thought desirable, it may be said, I am, in height, six feet four inches, nearly; lean in flesh ... no other marks or brands **recollected**."
2. Late in December 1859, Lincoln wrote a **brief** history of his life for a friend.
3. Thomas Lincoln was a **restless** man who moved his family often.
4. The Lincolns built a **crude** shelter made of logs.
5. Books and paper were **scarce** on the frontier.
6. Abe, Dennis, and the other farm boys would sit around and **swap** stories and jokes.

	WORD	PART OF SPEECH	DEFINITION
a.	______________	________	short, using few words
b.	______________	________	called back to mind; remembered
c.	______________	________	always agitated or in motion
d.	______________	________	simple; not fancy; lacking conveniences
e.	______________	________	to exchange or trade
f.	______________	________	hard to get; rare

B. Context Clues: Write the correct vocabulary word to complete each sentence. Use each word just once.

1. The shipwrecked sailors threw together a ______________ hut to shelter them from the rain.
2. The explorers went to the native village to see if they could ______________ some of their belongings for food.
3. The horses were nervous and ______________ as the lightning flashed and the thunder boomed outside the barn.

4. The note was ______________________, only three sentences long, so it didn't take long to read.

5. Dad made sure to fill the car's tank because he knew for the next 100 miles, gas

   stations were going to be ______________________.

6. Grandfather closed his eyes, searching his memory to see if he

   ______________________ anything else about the big hunting trip.

C. Characters: Identify the new characters introduced in Chapter 2. Then tell two things about each character.

1. Who was Abe Lincoln's father?

   ____

   ____

   ____

2. Who was Abe's sister?

   ____

   ____

   ____

3. Who became Abe's best friend?

   ____

   ____

   ____

4. Who was Abe's stepmother?

   ____

   ____

   ____

D. **Comprehension:** Answer the following questions in your own words using complete sentences. Use supporting details from the book where applicable.

1. a. Where did the family move after Lincoln's sister was born? b. Describe the home they built there. Give 3 details.

   a. ____

   ____

   b. ____

   ____

   ____

2. Compared to other families of that time, were the Lincolns considered to be poor? Give 2 examples.

   ____

   ____

   ____

3. a. What caused the death of Lincoln's mother? b. How did her death affect her children?

   a. ____

   ____

   b. ____

   ____

4. a. How old was Abe when his mother died? b. Where did Thomas Lincoln go after his wife's death? c. How did Abe's family life change when his father returned?

a. ______________________________

____

b. ______________________________

____

c. ______________________________

____

5. a. What did the Lincoln children think about Sarah Bush Johnston as a stepmother? b. How did she treat her stepchildren?

a. ______________________________

____

b. ______________________________

____

6. What efforts did Abe make to educate himself? Give 3 examples.

____

____

____

7. Describe the trip Lincoln took when he was seventeen. Give 3 details.

____

____

____

____

____

____

____

____

Name: ______________________ Date: ______________________

Chapter 3 "New Salem Years"

A. Vocabulary: Use the definitions and the vocabulary words below to fill in the crossword puzzle.

politics	campaign	debt	dismissed
legislature	militia	lawyer	plunged

Across

3. the work of government; its methods, tactics
4. a group that has the duty or power of making laws for a state or country
5. the competition by rival political candidates for public office
6. something owed to another

Down

1. put out of mind; stopped thinking about
2. army of citizens who are not regular soldiers but who undergo training for emergency duty or national defense
3. threw oneself into water, danger, a campaign, etc.
4. a person whose profession is giving advice about the laws or acting for others in a court of law

B. Context: Read each of the following sentences and name the part of speech (noun, verb, adverb, or adjective) for each vocabulary word. Then use each underlined vocabulary word in a new sentence.

1. As a clerk in Denton Offutt's store, Lincoln spent countless hours discussing **politics**.

   Part of Speech: ______________________________

   ____

   ____

2. Lincoln's **campaign** for the Illinois Legislature was interrupted by Chief Black Hawk's War.

   Part of Speech: ______________________________

   ____

   ____

3. Lincoln spent years working odd jobs in order to pay off his **debt**.

   Part of Speech: ______________________________

   ____

   ____

4. Although Lincoln had strong ambitions to become a lawyer, he **dismissed** the idea because of his lack of education.

   Part of Speech: ______________________________

   ____

   ____

5. When the governor of Illinois called for volunteers for the **militia**, Lincoln volunteered.

   Part of Speech: ______________________________

   ____

   ____

6. John Todd Stuart urged Lincoln to become a **lawyer**.

   Part of Speech: ______________________

   ____

   ____

7. Lincoln noted that many of the lawyers in the state **legislature** had never attended college.

   Part of Speech: ______________________

   ____

   ____

8. Once Lincoln returned to New Salem, the election was only two weeks away, so he **plunged** into the campaign.

   Part of Speech: ______________________

   ____

   ____

C. **Characters:** Identify the new characters introduced in Chapter 3. Then tell two things about each character.

1. Who hired Abe and two others to build a flatboat?

   ____

   ____

   ____

2. Who wrestled with Lincoln?

   ____

   ____

   ____

3. Who encouraged Lincoln to become a lawyer?

   ____

   ____

4. Who turned down Lincoln's marriage proposal?

____

____

____

D. **Comprehension:** Answer the following questions in your own words using complete sentences. Use supporting details from the book where applicable.

1. a. How old was Abe when his father moved? b. Describe how Abe looked then. Give 3 details.

   a. ____________________________________

   b. ____________________________________

   ____

   ____

2. Why was Abe Lincoln glad to get a job in New Salem? List 2 reasons.

   ____

   ____

   ____

   ____

3. Why was Lincoln well liked by members of a local group of men? Give 3 reasons.

   ____

   ____

   ____

   ____

   ____

   ____

   ____

4. a. Why did Lincoln seek out other residents of the town? b. Who were these residents and what did they do for Lincoln? List 2 members.

   a. ______________________________

   ____

   b. ______________________________

   ____

   ____

   ____

5. a. What caused Lincoln to have plenty of time on his hands at work? b. What happened to his job as a result?

   a. ______________________________

   ____

   b. ______________________________

   ____

6. What event interrupted Lincoln's first election attempt?

   ____

7. How did Lincoln feel after the election? Give 3 details.

   ____

   ____

   ____

8. a. What did Lincoln do to prepare to earn a law degree? b. What did he say was most vital to being successful?

   a. ______________________________

   ____

   b. ______________________________

   ____

Name: ______________________________ Date: ______________________________

Chapter 4 "Lincoln The Lawyer"

A. Vocabulary: Write the underlined vocabulary word next to its definition below. Then name the part of speech (noun, verb, adverb, or adjective) for each word.

1. The law firm of Stuart & Lincoln **prospered** in Springfield.
2. Illinois was divided into **circuits**. Each circuit was made up of several counties.
3. Lincoln was a gifted speaker. He was quick and bright as a **debater**.
4. Lincoln sought friendships among the well-to-do and **influential** **citizens** of Springfield.
5. Mary Todd was the daughter of a wealthy Kentucky **merchant** and banker.
6. Mary was used to **luxury** and having servants.
7. Abe gave Mary a ring that was engraved with *Love is **eternal**.*

	WORD	PART OF SPEECH	DEFINITION
a.	______________________	__________	important, powerful
b.	______________________	__________	routes within a territory
c.	______________________	__________	had success; flourished
d.	______________________	__________	a person who participates in formal arguments at public meetings
e.	______________________	__________	lasting throughout all time; forever
f.	______________________	__________	people who live in a city, state, or country
g.	______________________	__________	a person who buys and sells for profit; trader
h.	______________________	__________	the best and most expensive food, clothes, houses, furniture, and amusements

B. Word Play: Use a vocabulary word to complete the phrase. The relationship between the first two words is the same as the relationship between the third and fourth words. This is called an analogy.

Example: "Hot is to cold as winter is to ___summer___." Since the first two words are opposites, you need a word that is opposite of "winter" to complete the phrase.

circuits	prospered	influential	citizens	debater	merchant	luxury	eternal

1. Big is to large as extravagance is to ______________________.
2. Attic is to loft as powerful is to ______________________.
3. Sad is to cheerful as failed is to ______________________.
4. Hate is to love as temporary is to ______________________.
5. Decision is to jury as government is to ______________________.
6. Hop is to jump as routes are to ______________________.
7. Win is to team as profit is to ______________________.
8. Happy is to glad as arguer is to ______________________.

C. Characters: Identify the new characters introduced in Chapter 4. Then tell two things about each character.

1. At whose home did Lincoln meet his future wife?

____

____

____

2. Who was Elizabeth Edwards' younger sister?

____

____

____

3. Who was the Lincoln's first child?

____

____

____

4. Who did Lincoln ask to become his partner when he opened his own law firm?

____

____

____

D. Events/Sequence: Number the events from Chapter 4 in the order (sequence) they occurred.

_____ a. Lincoln met Mary Ann Todd.

_____ b. Robert Todd Lincoln was born.

_____ c. Lincoln opened his own law firm.

_____ d. Lincoln left New Salem forever.

_____ e. William H. Herndon became Lincoln's law partner.

_____ f. Lincoln joined John Todd Stuart's law firm.

_____ g. Mary Todd and Abraham Lincoln married.

_____ h. The Lincolns bought a house in Springfield.

_____ i. Lincoln received a license to practice law in Illinois.

_____ j. Lincoln rode "Old Tom" on the circuit.

_____ k. Lincoln was a leader in the Whig party.

_____ l. Lincoln was reelected to the state legislature.

_____ m. Edward Lincoln was born.

_____ n. Springfield became the capital of Illinois.

_____ o. Springfield had a population of 1,500 people.

_____ p. The Lincolns lived in a boardinghouse.

E. **Comprehension:** Answer the following questions in your own words using complete sentences. Use supporting details from the book where applicable.

1. Why did Lincoln leave New Salem?

____

____

____

2. Describe the city of Springfield at the time Lincoln moved there. Give 3 details.

____

____

____

3. The author states that "Lincoln was becoming a leading figure among the Whigs in the state legislature." What details did the author provide to support this statement? Give 2 details.

____

____

____

4. a. Lincoln was popular among what group of voters? b. Which other people did he seek out?

a. ____

____

____

b. ____

____

____

5. How were Lincoln and Mary Todd similar? Give 3 examples.

____

____

____

6. Why do you think Lincoln felt comfortable around Mary Todd?

____

____

7. Why did Mary Todd find it hard to adjust to being a wife? Give 2 reasons.

____

____

____

____

8. What problems did riding the circuit cause for Lincoln and his family? Give 2 problems.

____

____

____

____

9. Describe the law office in which Lincoln and Billy Herndon worked.

____

____

____

____

____

Name: ______________________ **Date:** ______________________

Chapter 5 "A Seat in Congress"

A. Vocabulary: Write the underlined vocabulary word next to its definition below. Then name the part of speech (noun, verb, adverb, or adjective) for each word.

1. After four terms in the state legislature, Lincoln wanted new worlds to **conquer**.
2. Lincoln's work as a **congressman** kept him busy.
3. The Democrats' goal was to seize Mexican **territory** for the United States.
4. Lincoln called the president "a miserably **perplexed** man."
5. In his speech, Seward discussed the issue of **slavery**, which he opposed.
6. Few people in the North owned slaves, and **opposition** to slavery developed there.
7. Big **plantations** in the South required large numbers of slaves to raise the crops.
8. The Mexicans signed a peace **treaty**, giving some of their land to the United States.

	WORD	PART OF SPEECH	DEFINITION
a.	______________	________	condition in which a person is owned by another
b.	______________	________	a formal agreement approved and signed between nations
c.	______________	________	troubled with doubt; puzzled; confused
d.	______________	________	land belonging to a government
e.	______________	________	action against; resistance
f.	______________	________	a member of Congress or the legislature, especially of the House of Representatives
g.	______________	________	to gain, win, or obtain by effort; overcoming obstacles or opposition; to be victorious
h.	______________	________	large farms on which crops were raised, often by workers who were kept there

B. Word Scramble: Use the clue to help you unscramble each vocabulary word.

treaty	congressman	plantations	opposition
territory	perplexed	conquer	slavery

1. **UCROQEN** ____________________ If you don't do this to your fears, they will beat you.

2. **TPSTALNAOIN** ____________________ In the South, these required a large number of slaves to do the work.

3. **DEPEEXLRP** ____________________ Some feel this way when they try to solve a brainteaser.

4. **ETYRAT** ____________________ If this is signed, a country might prevent a war.

5. **NOOPIPTIISO** ____________________ If this is started by a political party, a new law might not pass.

6. **YSAVRLE** ____________________ This practice made people work under harsh conditions for little or no pay.

7. **EYTRORTIR** ____________________ In 1848, Oregon was not yet officially a state, but was one of these.

8. **NRNGCOASESM** ____________________ Lincoln was elected one of these.

C. Characters: Identify the new characters introduced in Chapter 5. Then tell two things about each character.

1. Who did Lincoln call "a miserably perplexed man?"

____

____

____

____

____

2. Who did Lincoln campaign for in the 1848 election?

3. With whom did Lincoln share the speaker's platform in Boston?

D. **Comprehension:** Answer the following questions in your own words using complete sentences. Use supporting details from the book where applicable.

1. a. Despite his success, how did Lincoln's feelings about being a legislator change in 1846? b. What did he do?

   a.

   b.

2. a. How did Mary Lincoln feel about life in the nation's capital? b. What did she do as a result?

   a.

   b.

3. Why did Lincoln oppose the Mexican War? Give 2 examples.

4. What did the United States gain under the terms of the treaty at the end of the Mexican War?

5. What caused slavery to spread in the South?

6. How did Lincoln expect to benefit from helping General Zachary Taylor win the presidential election in 1848?

7. Why did Lincoln reject the new job opportunity?

Name: ______________________ **Date:** ______________________

Chapter 6 "Turning Point" Part 1

A. Vocabulary: Write the underlined vocabulary word next to its definition below. Then name the part of speech (noun, verb, adverb, or adjective) for each word.

1. The firm of Lincoln & Herndon occupied two **cluttered** rooms on the second floor.
2. Lincoln could present a **complex** matter in easy-to-understand language.
3. Lincoln had to put up with many **hardships** while riding the circuits.
4. Lincoln began to represent railroads and big **corporations** in lawsuits.
5. An Illinois **journalist** placed Lincoln at the head of the law **profession** in the state.
6. Although the Lincolns nursed Eddie for two months, their efforts were in **vain**, Eddie died.
7. Lincoln said, "It is my pleasure that my children are free and happy, and unrestrained by parental **tyranny**."

	WORD	PART OF SPEECH	DEFINITION
a.	____________	______	messy; littered with things; in disorder
b.	____________	______	suffering; troubles
c.	____________	______	unsuccessful
d.	____________	______	hard to understand
e.	____________	______	large companies established by one or more people
f.	____________	______	cruel or unjust use of power
g.	____________	______	a writer for newspapers and magazines
h.	____________	______	an occupation requiring training and study

B. Synonym Chart: Write a vocabulary word that is a synonym to the words listed in the chart.

complex journalist profession vain corporations tyranny hardships cluttered

Synonym	Vocabulary Word
1. career	
2. untidy	
3. reporter	
4. complicated	
5. pointless	
6. businesses	
7. difficulties	
8. dictatorship	

C. Comprehension: Answer the following questions in your own words using complete sentences. Use supporting details from the book where applicable.

1. Number Lincoln's usual morning activities in the order (sequence) they occurred.

_____ a. stopped to chat with friends and other lawyers

_____ b. fed and groomed his horse

_____ c. awakened at dawn

_____ d. had breakfast with Mary and the two boys

_____ e. arrived at office

_____ f. left for the office

_____ g. cut firewood

2. How did Lincoln and Herndon divide up their work responsibilities?

___

___

___

3. What challenges did Lincoln face while riding the circuit? Give 3 details.

___

___

___

4. a. Lincoln was becoming recognized for what trait? b. How did people refer to him because of this?

a. ___

___

b. ___

___

5. What two losses did the Lincoln family experience from 1849 to 1851?

___

___

___

___

6. Did the birth of the Lincolns' third child, William, ease Mary's heartache? Give at least 1 detail.

___

___

___

___

7. a. What nickname did Lincoln give his fourth son? b. Why did he call him this?

   a. ____

   ____

   b. ____

   ____

   ____

8. a. What were the Lincolns' thoughts on making children behave? b. How did Billy Herndon, Lincoln's law partner, feel about the Lincolns' children?

   a. ____

   ____

   ____

   ____

   b. ____

   ____

   ____

   ____

Name: ______________________ **Date:** ______________________

Chapter 6 "Turning Point" Part 2

A. Vocabulary: Write the underlined vocabulary word next to its definition below. Then name the part of speech (noun, verb, adverb, or adjective) for each word.

1. A **vast** area was affected by the Kansas-Nebraska Act.
2. Slavery had long been banned in the new territories by the Missouri **Compromise**.
3. Lincoln called the new law a "great moral wrong and **injustice**."
4. The Kansas-Nebraska Act could **trigger** new growth in slavery.
5. Douglas worked hard in getting the Senate to pass the **bill**.
6. Lincoln and Douglas had often argued about **issues**.
7. The **extension** of slavery was wrong, Lincoln declared.

	WORD	PART OF SPEECH	DEFINITION
a.	______________	________	to set off; start
b.	______________	________	a proposed law presented to a lawmaking group for its approval
c.	______________	________	continuation; increase
d.	______________	________	a settlement of differences in which both sides agree to give up part of what each demands
e.	______________	________	violation; unfair act
f.	______________	________	points to be debated; problems
g.	______________	________	very large; immense

B. Synonyms in Context: Substitute a vocabulary word for each underlined word.

vast	compromise	issues	trigger	injustice	bill	extension

1. When Congress passed the Kansas-Nebraska Act in 1854, an enormous area was changed. ____________________

2. Lincoln felt the expansion of slavery was wrong. ____________________

3. Stephen Douglas supported the Kansas-Nebraska Act. He wanted the Senate to pass the proposed law. ____________________

4. Lincoln thought the Kansas-Nebraska Act might start new growth for slavery.

   ____

5. Regarding slavery, some legislators felt that it was necessary to reach an agreement on the issue. ____________________

6. Lincoln and Douglas often disagreed on important matters. ____________________

7. Lincoln felt the Kansas-Nebraska Act was a great moral wrong and promoted inequality. ____________________

C. Characters: Identify a new character introduced in Chapter 6. Then tell two things about the character.

Who was the U.S. senator from Illinois who often argued with Lincoln about the issues?

____

____

____

D. **Summary:** A summary is a brief account of the main points. Using complete sentences, summarize this book from Chapter 1 through Chapter 6.

E. Comprehension: Answer the following questions in your own words using complete sentences. Use supporting details from the book where applicable.

1. a. What new law interrupted Lincoln's contentment? b. What right did the act give to some people?

   a. ______________________________

   ____

   b. ______________________________

   ____

2. This act could have had a much longer name. Based on the areas affected, what could it have been called?

   ____

   ____

   ____

   ____

3. How did this act impact the growth of slavery in the country?

   ____

   ____

   ____

4. a. How did Lincoln feel when he heard about the Kansas-Nebraska Act?
   b. What did he have to say about it?

   a. ______________________________

   ____

   ____

   ____

   b. ______________________________

   ____

   ____

5. Stephen Douglas, a United States senator from Illinois, and Lincoln had different points of view about the Kansas-Nebraska Act. How were their points of view different?

   Douglas' view: ______________________________

   ____

   ____

   Lincoln's view: ______________________________

   ____

   ____

6. Most Southerners and Northerners disagreed about slavery. How were their points of view different?

   Northerners: ______________________________

   ____

   ____

   ____

   Southerners: ______________________________

   ____

   ____

   ____

7. Along with these different opinions came strong feelings of anger on both sides. This anger and outrage helped fuel what historic event?

   ____

   ____

   ____

   ____

Name: ______________________ **Date:** ______________________

Chapter 7 "Losing Effort"

A. Vocabulary: Write the underlined vocabulary word next to its definition below. Then name the part of speech (noun, verb, adverb, or adjective) for each word.

1. The Supreme Court said that Congress had no right to **prohibit** slavery.
2. Republicans thought the Dred Scott decision was cruel, **inhumane**, and unfair.
3. Lincoln accepted the Republican **nomination** for the United States Senate.
4. "I believe this government cannot **endure**, permanently half slave and half free."
5. "I do not expect the Union to be **dissolved** ... but I do expect that it will cease to be divided."
6. After the being defeated in the Senate election, Lincoln became **gloomy**.

	WORD	PART OF SPEECH	DEFINITION
a.	______________	________	lacking in kindness, mercy, or tenderness
b.	______________	________	to put up with; bear; last
c.	______________	________	ended; broken up
d.	______________	________	selection for office or duty; appointment to office or duty
e.	______________	________	in low spirits; sad; melancholy
f.	______________	________	to forbid by law or authority

B. Context: Use each vocabulary word in a sentence.

1. ____

____

2. ____

____

3. ____

____

4. ______________________________

____

5. ______________________________

____

6. ______________________________

____

C. Characters: Identify the new characters introduced in Chapter 7. Then tell two things about each character.

1. What member of the Republican Party did Lincoln support in the 1856 presidential election?"

____

____

____

2. What was the name of the slave who sued for his freedom?

____

____

____

D. Comprehension: Answer the following questions in your own words using complete sentences. Use supporting details from the book where applicable.

1. a. After the passage of the Kansas-Nebraska Act, what new party did Lincoln and others join? b. How did this new party feel about slavery?

a. ______________________________

____

b. ______________________________

____

____

2. a. How did the Supreme Court rule in the Dred Scott decision? b. How did the court explain that decision? Give 2 reasons.

   a. ______________________________

   ____

   ____

   b. ______________________________

   ____

   ____

3. a. How did Lincoln respond to the court's decision? b. What did he say that helps us understand his reaction?

   a. ______________________________

   ____

   ____

   b. ______________________________

   ____

   ____

4. What did Lincoln say the Republican Party must do? Give 2 details.

   ____

   ____

   ____

5. a. How did Lincoln feel after the 1858 Senate election? b. Why did he feel this way?

   a. ______________________________

   ____

   b. ______________________________

   ____

E. **Compare/Contrast:** A Venn diagram uses circles to show similarities and differences. Using information from Chapter 7, write:

- 4 details about Abraham Lincoln that made him different from Stephen Douglas
- 4 details about Stephen Douglas that made him different from Abraham Lincoln
- 3 details that show what both men had in common

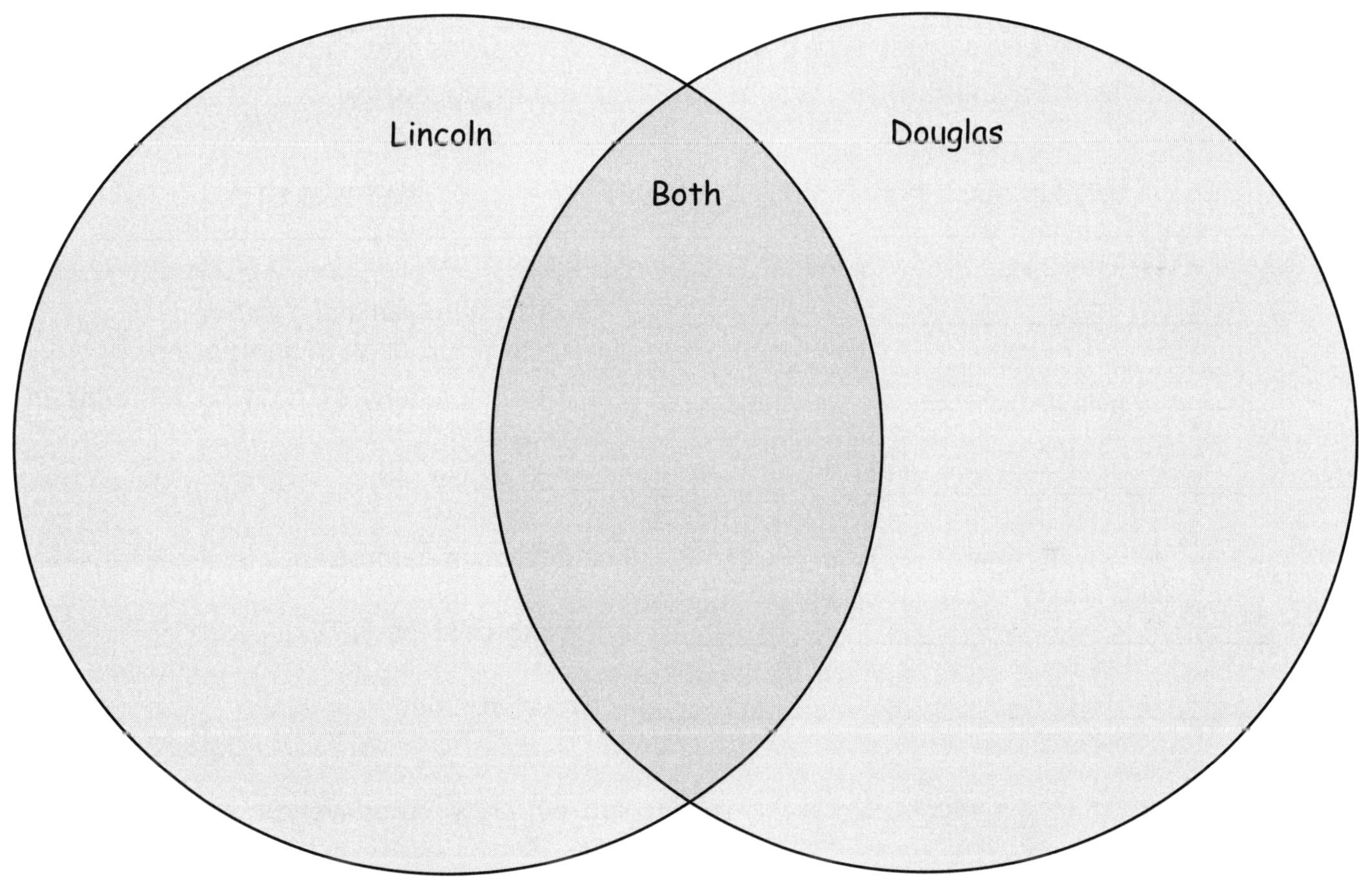

Name: ______________________ Date: ______________________

Chapter 8 "The People's Choice"

A. Vocabulary: Write the underlined vocabulary word next to its definition below. Then name the part of speech (noun, verb, adverb, or adjective) for each word.

1. Lincoln's **ambitions** were still focused on the Senate.
2. Republican leaders **launched** a Lincoln-for-president campaign.
3. Republicans should not be afraid to **oppose** the extension of slavery.
4. The Southern states were urged to **secede** from the Union if Lincoln became president.
5. Even before Lincoln was sworn in as president, he was facing a **severe** test.
6. Lincoln left Springfield for Washington for his **inauguration**.

	WORD	PART OF SPEECH	DEFINITION
a.	______________	________	to withdraw formally from membership in an organization
b.	______________	________	act or ceremony of putting someone in office
c.	______________	________	strict; hard
d.	______________	________	started on a course
e.	______________	________	strong desires for success
f.	______________	________	to act against

B. Which Word: Use a vocabulary word to find out which word or words is described.

1. Which word is an antonym of lenient? ______________________
2. Which word is a synonym of quit? ______________________
3. Which word is an antonym of indifference? ______________________
4. Which word is a synonym of installation? ______________________
5. Which word is an antonym of stopped?______________________
6. Which word is a synonym of resist? ______________________

C. Comprehension: Answer the following questions in your own words using complete sentences. Use supporting details from the book where applicable.

1. What positive effect did the debates with Stephen Douglas have for Lincoln?

____

____

____

2. Why do you think Lincoln didn't try to prevent the Republican leaders from launching a presidential campaign?

____

____

____

____

3. Summarize Lincoln's New York speech.

____

____

____

____

____

____

4. a. After Lincoln won the election, what challenge awaited him? b. Why did he think no states would secede? c. Was he right?

a. ____

____

b. ____

____

c. ____

____

5. a. Which state was the first to secede? b. What were the next five states to leave the Union?

a. ____

____

b. ____

____

Name: ______________________________ Date: ________________________________

Chapter 9 "The White House at War"

A. Vocabulary: Use the definitions and the vocabulary words below to fill in the crossword puzzle.

wounded	parts	industrial	crisis
occasionally	fleet	urgent	surrender

Down

2. now and then; once in a while
4. to give up and quit fighting
6. a large group of ships

Across

1. suffering from an injury
3. places where ships can load and unload goods
5. disaster, trouble
7. having highly developed manufacturing businesses
8. very important; demanding immediate action or attention

B. Context: Read each of the following sentences and name the part of speech (noun, verb, adverb, or adjective) for each vocabulary word. Then use each underlined vocabulary word in a new sentence.

1. On Lincoln's first night as president, an **urgent** letter awaited his attention.

   Part of Speech: ______________________________

   ____

   ____

2. The Confederates learned the **fleet** was on the way.

   Part of Speech: ______________________________

   ____

   ____

3. Shock and anger swept the North after Fort Sumter's **surrender**.

   Part of Speech: ______________________________

   ____

   ____

4. ... that Union warships would begin stopping all vessels from entering or leaving Southern **ports**.

   Part of Speech: ______________________________

   ____

   ____

5. The North had greater **industrial** strength.

   Part of Speech: ______________________________

   ____

   ____

6. They called for a major battle that would end the **crisis**.

   Part of Speech: ______________________________

   ____

   ____

7. In the evening, the Lincolns would **occasionally** attend the theater.

   Part of Speech: ______________________________

   ____

   ____

8. More than 13,000 troops were killed or **wounded**.

   Part of Speech: ______________________________

   ____

   ____

C. **Events/Sequence:** Number the events from Chapter 9 in the order (sequence) they occurred.

_____ a. Union troops met up with Confederate forces at Bull Run.

_____ b. Virginia, Arkansas, North Carolina, and Tennessee joined the Confederacy.

_____ c. The war was in its second year.

_____ d. Lincoln called for 75,000 volunteers for the army.

_____ e. Lincoln's first night as president

_____ f. Willie died of a fever.

_____ g. Ships were sent to Fort Sumter loaded with supplies.

_____ h. Union forces captured New Orleans.

_____ i. Confederate guns opened fire on Fort Sumter.

_____ j. Northern forces lost 13,000 troops at Shiloh.

_____ k. A blockade by Union warships stopped all vessels from entering or leaving Southern ports.

_____ l. The Union army retreated from Richmond.

_____ m. A letter arrived from General Robert Anderson.

D. Characters: Identify the new characters introduced in Chapter 9. Then tell two things about each character.

1. Who was the commander of the U.S. troops at Fort Sumter, North Carolina?

___

___

___

2. Who forced the Union army to retreat in the summer of 1862?

___

___

___

E. Comprehension: Answer the following questions in your own words using complete sentences. Use supporting details from the book where applicable.

1. No sooner had he been elected president, then Lincoln faced a big challenge. What was it?

___

___

2. Why was Lincoln's decision difficult? Give 2 reasons.

___

___

___

___

3. Did Lincoln arrive at a decision right away? Give 2 details.

___

___

___

___

4. a. How did Lincoln force the Confederates to strike the first blow in the war?

5. When the Civil War began, which side, the North or the South, was better prepared? Give 2 details.

6. a. Why did Lincoln push the Union army into the first big battle of the war?
   b. What two effects did the outcome have on Northerners?

   a.

   b.

7. The Lincolns' sons pretty much ran wild at home. Give 3 details.

8. How did Lincoln react after two years of war, many battle defeats and large numbers of casualties?

____

____

____

Name: ______________________ **Date:** ______________________

Chapter 10 "Freeing The Slaves"

A. **Vocabulary**: Write the underlined vocabulary word next to its definition below. Then name the part of speech (noun, verb, adverb, or adjective) for each word.

1. The border states were not in **rebellion** against the United States.
2. Lincoln worked out a plan that would **emancipate** the nation's slaves.
3. The Emancipation Proclamation was a **symbol** of freedom.
4. Lincoln called for a constitutional **amendment** that would end slavery.
5. The Thirteenth Amendment was **ratified** by the states on December 18, 1865.
6. The amendment **outlawed** slavery in every part of America forever.

	WORD	PART OF SPEECH	DEFINITION
a.	______________	________	a change or addition made to a law or a bill
b.	______________	________	approved; passed; confirmed
c.	______________	________	to set free
d.	______________	________	armed resistance or fight against a government; a revolt
e.	______________	________	something representing something else
f.	______________	________	declared illegal

B. Word Play: Use a vocabulary word to complete the analogy.

amendment	ratified	outlawed	emancipate	rebellion	symbol

1. Tiny is to small as uprising is to ____________________.
2. Cloudy is to sunny as enslave is to ____________________.
3. Happy is to merry as sign is to ____________________.
4. Cheery is to blissful as correction is to ____________________.
5. Slow is to fast as disapproved is to ____________________.
6. Sweet is to sour as allowed is to ____________________.

C. Comprehension: Answer the following questions in your own words using complete sentences. Use supporting details from the book where applicable.

1. Do you think Lincoln was calm and persistent? Give 2 details.

____

____

____

____

2. a. Why didn't Lincoln try to force the South to give up slavery in the early stages of the Civil War? b. What did he think would happen if the Union army was victorious?

a. ____________________

____

____

b. ____________________

____

____

3. a. Why did Lincoln think the two sides were fighting in the Civil War? b. What did some members of Congress believe was the cause?

   a. ____

   ____

   b. ____

   ____

4. a. What states especially concerned Lincoln? b. What were they called? c. What did they have in common with the South?

   a. ____

   ____

   b. ____

   ____

   c. ____

   ____

5. What did Lincoln think would be the risk to freeing the slaves?

   ____

   ____

6. What did the Emancipation Proclamation do?

   ____

   ____

7. Were all slaves freed by the Emancipation Proclamation? Give 2 examples.

   ____

   ____

   ____

8. a. Why did Lincoln push for the Thirteenth Amendment? b. What did it do?

a. ____

____

b. ____

____

Name: ______________________ **Date:** ______________________

Chapter 11 "Gettysburg"

A. Vocabulary: Write the underlined vocabulary word next to its definition below. Then name the part of speech (noun, verb, adverb, or adjective) for each word.

1. Heavy losses on the battlefield was the reason many soldiers **deserted** their units.
2. To bring new recruits, the government decided to **draft** young men for the army.
3. In the North, Lincoln's **policies** and programs triggered great **discontent**
4. Lincoln sought ways to cope with citizen **unrest**.
5. The **climax** of the Battle of Gettysburg came on the afternoon of July 3, 1863.
6. As Lincoln sat down, the audience applauded **politely**.
7. The war was about more than the Union, it was also about **equality**.

	WORD	PART OF SPEECH	DEFINITION
a.	______________	________	in a way that shows good manners; properly
b.	______________	________	sameness in number, value, or rank; being equal
c.	______________	________	abandoned; left
d.	______________	________	highest or most intense part
e.	______________	________	select somebody to enter the army
f.	______________	________	plans of action; rules
g.	______________	________	uneasy feeling; dissatisfaction
h.	______________	________	lack of ease and quiet; restlessness almost to the point of rebellion

B. Word Scramble: Use the clue to help you unscramble each vocabulary word.

deserted draft equality policies discontent politely unrest climax

1. **FTADR** ____________________ The government wanted men between the ages of 18-25 for the war.

2. **RNETSU** ____________________ This sometimes leads to a revolution.

3. **REETDDES** ____________________ Left or ran away from duty.

4. **ELTIPOYL** ____________________ If you ask for something this way, you may receive it.

5. **LMICXA** ____________________ His career reached this when he was elected president.

6. **LIISEPOC** ____________________ A school notifies students of these at the beginning of each year.

7. **TEUQLYIA** ____________________ Democracy provides this opportunity for all citizens.

8. **TNNSIODCTE** ____________________ This is a feeling of uneasiness.

C. Characters: Identify the new characters introduced in Chapter 11. Then tell two things about each character.

1. Which general did not try to stop the advance of Lee's army?

____

____

____

2. Who did Lincoln choose to replace General Hooker?

____

____

____

3. Who gave the principal address at the dedication of the National Soldiers' Cemetery at Gettysburg?

____

____

D. Comprehension: Answer the following questions in your own words using complete sentences. Use supporting details from the book where applicable.

1. After two years of the war, was Lincoln satisfied with the Union army commanders? Give 2 examples.

____

____

____

2. a. Why was the Union army short on soldiers? Give 2 examples. b. What did the government do to get more soldiers for the army?

a. ____

____

____

b. ____

____

____

3. a. How did most Southerners feel about African Americans serving in the Confederate army? b. Why did they feel this way?

a. ____

____

____

b. ____

____

____

4. a. What were Lincoln's practices that upset many people in the North? b. What was Lincoln's reaction?

   a. ______________________________

   ____

   b. ______________________________

   ____

5. Give three details about the great battle that took place in southern Pennsylvania.

   ____

   ____

   ____

   ____

6. Why was the Union victory at Gettysburg important? Give 2 reasons.

   ____

   ____

7. What year and event did Lincoln refer to in the first line of his Gettysburg Address?

   ____

   ____

   ____

   ____

8. Why did Lincoln doubt his Gettysburg Address had much of an impact? Give 2 details.

   ____

   ____

   ____

   ____

Name: ______________________ Date: ______________________

Chapter 12 "With Charity for All"

A. Vocabulary: Write the underlined vocabulary word next to its definition below. Then name the part of speech (noun, verb, adverb, or adjective) for each word.

1. Grant was pressing the enemy hard, but his **tactics** had cost many lives.
2. At the Capitol, Lincoln took his **oath** of office a second time
3. As the Yankees invaded the South, conditions there had become **desperate**.
4. Lincoln was curious to visit the now-**battered** city of Richmond.
5. "With **malice** toward none; with **charity** for all ... "
6. " ... let us **strive** on to finish the work we are in ... "

	WORD	PART OF SPEECH	DEFINITION
a.	______________	________	having little chance for hope; hopeless
b	______________	________	desire to inflict injury, harm, or suffering
c.	______________	________	damaged by hard use or violence; wrecked
d.	______________	________	generosity toward others
e.	______________	________	ways to attempt to gain advantage or success; methods
f.	______________	________	to try hard
g.	______________	________	a solemn promise

B. Antonyms: Put a line through the word that is an antonym to the vocabulary word.

Vocabulary Word	Choice 1	Choice 2	Choice 3
1. oath	pledge	lie	vow
2. tactics	guesswork	strategy	plans
3. battered	crumbling	rebuilt	damaged
4. desperate	hopeless	rash	confident
5. malice	bitterness	hatred	kindness
6. charity	goodness	hatred	affection
7. strive	fight	struggle	quit

C. Characters: Identify the new characters introduced in Chapter 12. Then tell two things about each character.

1. When Lincoln said, "I like that man. He fights," to whom was he referring?

____

____

____

2. Who did the Democrats choose to run against Lincoln in 1864?

____

____

____

D. Comprehension: Answer the following questions in your own words using complete sentences. Use supporting details from the book where applicable.

1. What strategy did Lincoln and Grant use to overwhelm General Lee and the Southern armies?

____

____

____

2. How did they carry out the plan? Give 2 details to support your answer.

____

____

____

____

3. Why did Lincoln want to win the presidential election of 1864? Give 2 reasons.

____

____

____

4. Why did Lincoln worry that he might be unable to beat the Democrats' candidate? Give 2 reasons.

____

____

____

____

5. What were two positive effects of the Union battlefield successes?

____

____

____

____

6. How was Lincoln's second inauguration speech similar to his address at Gettysburg? Give 3 similarities.

____

____

____

____

____

____

7. Give 2 examples of the heavy impact the war was having on the South by early 1865.

____

____

____

____

8. a. Why did Lincoln want to visit the capital of the Confederacy? b. What did Lincoln and his son, Tad, see there? Give 3 details.

a. ____

____

b. ____

____

____

____

____

____

Name: ______________________ Date: ______________________

Chapter 13
"I Know I'm in Danger"

A. Vocabulary: Write the underlined vocabulary word next to its definition below. Then name the part of speech (noun, verb, adverb, or adjective) for each word.

1. Hardly a day went by that Lincoln did not receive a **threatening** letter.
2. **Routine** tasks occupied him.
3. The orchestra **saluted** Lincoln by playing "Hail to the Chief."
4. At the play, the Lincolns sat with Henry Rathbone and Clara Harris, to whom he was **engaged**.
5. Lincoln enjoyed the play and laughed **heartily**.
6. The **unconscious** Lincoln was carried from the theater.
7. A friend of Mary's convinced her to rest in the **parlor**.
8. Four of the people who plotted to assassinate Lincoln were eventually **convicted**.

	WORD	PART OF SPEECH	DEFINITION
a.	______________	________	causing alarm; a warning of danger
b.	______________	________	regular, ordinary
c.	______________	________	promised or pledged to marry
d.	______________	________	energetically; sincerely
e.	______________	________	honored; welcomed
f.	______________	________	found guilty
g.	______________	________	a room in a house for relaxing
h.	______________	________	not able to feel or think

B. Synonym/Antonym: Write the vocabulary word that is a synonym and an antonym of the words given.

saluted routine unconscious threatening heartily engaged parlor convicted

Synonym	Antonym	Vocabulary Word
1. intimidating	soothing	
2. comatose	awake	
3. regular	special	
4. energetically	feebly	
5. greeted	ignored	
6. room	outdoors	
7. guilty	innocent	
8. unavailable	free	

C. Characters: Identify the new characters introduced in Chapter 13. Then tell two things about each character.

1. Who were the man and woman seated with the Lincolns at Ford's Theatre?

____

____

____

____

2. What was the name of Lincoln's attacker?

____

____

____

____

D. **Comprehension:** Answer the following questions in your own words using complete sentences. Use supporting details from the book where applicable.

1. What news did Lincoln receive when he steamed back to Washington?

____

____

____

2. a. How did Lincoln feel about the news? b. How did he show that?

   a. ____

   ____

   ____

   b. ____

   ____

   ____

3. a. What did many Northern government officials want to do to the Confederate leaders? b. Did Lincoln feel the same way? Give 2 details.

   a. ____

   ____

   ____

   b. ____

   ____

   ____

4. Why were Lincoln's advisors concerned about his welfare?

____

____

____

____

5. What happened after one of the actors caused the audience to burst out laughing at Ford's Theatre? Summarize five important events in order.

   a. ______________________________

   ____

   b. ______________________________

   ____

   c. ______________________________

   ____

   d. ______________________________

   ____

   e. ______________________________

   ____

6. Where did the president die?

   ____

   ____

7. a. How did people react during the journey of the funeral train? b. Where was Lincoln buried?

   a. ______________________________

   ____

   ____

   ____

   ____

   b. ______________________________

   ____

   ____

Name: ______________________ Date: ______________________

Chapter 14 "Lincoln Remembered"

A. Vocabulary: Write the underlined vocabulary word next to its definition below. Then name the part of speech (noun, verb, adverb, or adjective) for each word.

1. Houses, shops, and buildings were decorated with black ribbon or other signs of **mourning**.
2. Many hundreds of monuments and memorials would be **erected** in Lincoln's honor.
3. A **towering** shaft of granite, it was dedicated in Springfield, Illinois, in 1874.
4. The memorial is an **awesome** tribute to the sixteenth president.
5. Within months after Lincoln's death, written **accounts** of his life began to appear.
6. Billions of pennies are **minted** each year.
7. When first issued, the coin drew some **complaints**.
8. Lincoln's name has come to **indicate** honesty.

	WORD	PART OF SPEECH	DEFINITION
a.	______________	________	stand for; represent
b.	______________	________	constructed in a vertical position
c.	______________	________	statements of facts or events
d.	______________	________	wonderful; admirable
e.	______________	________	impressively high or great
f.	______________	________	objections; protests
g.	______________	________	coined; produced
h.	______________	________	sadness or grieving caused by a death

B. Word Play: Use a vocabulary word to complete the analogy.

mourning	erected	towering	awesome	accounts	minted	complaints	indicate

1. Hot is to cold as stunted is to ______________________.
2. Full is to empty as happiness is to ______________________.
3. Completed is to finished as coined is to ______________________.
4. Gifts are to presents as statements are to ______________________.
5. Walk is to stroll as amazing is to ______________________.
6. Sweet is to sour as demolished is to ______________________.
7. Shout is to whisper as compliments are to ______________________.
8. Joyous is to cheerful as suggest is to______________________.

C. Comprehension: Answer the following questions in your own words using complete sentences. Use supporting details from the book where applicable.

1. How did the nation react to Lincoln's death? Give 3 examples.

____

____

____

____

2. a. Why did some people disapprove of Lincoln's image appearing on the penny?
   b. How did the people who supported the idea feel?

   a. ____

   ____

   b. ____

   ____

3. Where else does Lincoln's likeness appear? Give 3 places.

____

____

____

4. Why do many financial institutions use Lincoln's name?

____

____

____

Name: ______________________ Date: ______________________

Events/Sequence for Abraham Lincoln

Write the year these events happened in Abraham Lincoln's life. Then list the lettered events in the order (sequence) they occurred. Be careful; some years have more than one event, so you'll have to know the months they occurred to get them in the right order.

Year	Event	Order
1809	Abraham Lincoln is born.	1st
______	Civil War begins	______
______	Receives license as lawyer	______
______	Elected president of the United States	______
______	Dies in Washington, D.C.	______
______	Re-elected president	______
______	Loses to Stephen Douglas in Senate election	______
______	Marries Mary Todd	______
______	Delivers Gettysburg Address	______
______	Elected to the Illinois Legislature	______
______	Shot by John Wilkes Booth	______
______	Issues Emancipation Proclamation	______
______	Civil War ends	______
______	Elected to the U.S. House of Representatives	______
______	Serves as volunteer in Black Hawk's War	______
______	Inaugurated as 16th president of the United States	______

Name: ______________________ Date: ______________________

Compare/Contrast Writing Paper
Introduction

After reading George Sullivan's book, "In Their Own Words: Abraham Lincoln," go back and re-read the chapters featuring Abraham Lincoln and Stephen Douglas. While reading the chapters, use a pencil and paper to take notes on any differences and similarities you notice between the two men.

Your notes will make it much easier to write your compare/contrast paper on Lincoln and Douglas. Good, detailed notes smooth the transition to pre-writing and improve the overall quality of your paper. Use the notes to help complete the pre-writing sheet.

Name: ______________________ Date: ______________________

Compare/Contrast Pre-Write
Abraham Lincoln and Stephen Douglas
Character Trait* List

Abraham Lincoln	Stephen Douglas
Trait	Trait

*a distinguishing characteristic or quality

Name: ______________________________ **Date:** ______________________________

Compare/Contrast 1st Draft Directions
Abraham Lincoln and Stephen Douglas

Directions: Use a separate piece of paper to write 4 paragraphs using the instructions below. Do not use I, me, my, myself, our, we, you, your, or any other first or second person pronouns in your first 3 paragraphs. Examples of topic sentences are on the next page.

Title: ____

Paragraph 1: Write an introduction stating what you are comparing and contrasting.

a. Get your audience interested in reading your paper.
b. Give official title, background of individuals and how they know each other.
c. 3 or more sentences

Paragraph 2: Compare the similarities between Abraham Lincoln and Stephen Douglas.

a. Write a topic sentence about how they are alike. (see p. 57)
b. Give at least 3 traits to support how they are the same.
c. Give examples of events from the book that support the traits.
d. 4 or more sentences

Paragraph 3: Contrast the differences between Abraham Lincoln and Stephen Douglas.

a. Write a topic sentence about how they are different. (see p. 57)
b. Give at least 3 traits to support how they are different.
c. Give examples of events from the book that support the traits.
c. 4 or more sentences

Paragraph 4: Close the paper by bringing your ideas together.

a. Use at least one of the following conclusion strategies:
    - Summarize the main points.
    - Draw a conclusion about what you learned writing this paper— are Lincoln and Douglas more alike or different?
    - Give your opinion on the two.
b. 2 or more sentences

Name: ______________________________ Date: ________________________________

Compare/Contrast
Examples of Topic Sentences
Abraham Lincoln and Stephen Douglas

Comparing

1. Abraham Lincoln and Stephen Douglas have many similarities.
2. Abraham Lincoln and Stephen Douglas have many characteristics in common.
3. Abraham Lincoln and Stephen Douglas are alike in many ways.
4. Abraham Lincoln and Stephen Douglas are the same in many ways.
5. Abraham Lincoln and Stephen Douglas resemble each other in many different ways.
6. Abraham Lincoln and Stephen Douglas have a few similarities.

Contrasting

1. Abraham Lincoln and Stephen Douglas have many differences.
2. Abraham Lincoln and Stephen Douglas are unlike each other.
3. Abraham Lincoln and Stephen Douglas are opposite in many ways.
4. Abraham Lincoln and Stephen Douglas do not have many differences.
5. Abraham Lincoln and Stephen Douglas have few differences.

Name: ______________________ **Date:** ______________________

Compare/Contrast
Editing (CUPS) 1st Draft
Abraham Lincoln and Stephen Douglas

Directions: First, by yourself, make all the necessary changes in red on your first draft. **Reread each paragraph 4 times** checking for the following corrections:

1. *CAPITAL LETTERS*
2. *WORD USAGE*
3. *PUNCTUATION*
4. *SPELLING.*

Next, have a partner give you suggestions and initial each part as you complete it together.

	Introduction Paragraph	Comparing Paragraph	Contrasting Paragraph	Closing Paragraph
"C"apital Letters	You	You	You	You
	Partner	Partner	Partner	Partner
Word "U"sage	You	You	You	You
	Partner	Partner	Partner	Partner
"P"unctuation	You	You	You	You
	Partner	Partner	Partner	Partner
"S"pelling	You	You	You	You
	Partner	Partner	Partner	Partner

Now write your final draft. Make sure to include your editing changes.

Name: ____________________ **Date:** ____________________

Compare/Contrast Paper Grade Sheet
Abraham Lincoln and Stephen Douglas

(Put in the grading scale used on progress report card from the school.)

________ Plans and composes writing

________ Revises writing

________ Edits writing

________ Communicates effectively using written language

________ Applies spelling strategies to independent work

________ Creates legible documents using cursive writing

Grading Scale

______=__________

______=__________

______=__________

______=__________

______=__________

Use the checklist below to help score the writing project

______ Did not use the pronouns *I, me, my, mine, myself, our, we, you, your,* or any other 1st or 2nd person pronouns in the 1st three paragraphs.

______ Four paragraphs

1st Paragraph: Introductory Paragraph

______ 3 sentences (at least)

______ Introduced who or what you were going to compare and contrast.

______ Got your audience interested in reading your paper.

______ Gave official titles/background of individuals and how they knew each other.

2nd Paragraph: Comparing Paragraph

______ 4 sentences (at least)

______ Topic sentence about how they were alike.

______ Supporting details: Told how they were the same. (at least 3 traits)

______ Gave examples of events from the book that supported the traits.

3rd Paragraph: Contrasting Paragraph

______ 4 sentences (at least)

______ Topic sentence about how they were different.

______ Supporting details: Told how they were different. (at least 3 traits)

______ Gave examples of events from the book that supported the traits.

4th Paragraph: Closing Paragraph

______ 2 sentences (at least)

______ Brought ideas together letting the readers know you were concluding your paper.

______ 1. Summarized the main points.

______ 2. Drew a conclusion. (What was learned writing the paper—are Mr. Lincoln and Mr. Douglas more alike or different?)

______ 3. Gave your opinion on how the individuals compared and contrasted.

Name: ______________________________ **Date:** ______________________________

Reading Detective®

Directions: Read the following passage and the Gettysburg Address. Then answer the questions on the next page.

[1]The Civil War had been raging for more than two years, with neither the North nor the South approaching victory, when the two armies met in a great battle near the town of Gettysburg, Pennsylvania. [2]The fighting was fierce and both sides suffered many deaths and injuries.

[3]On November 19, 1863, Lincoln went to Gettysburg to speak at the dedication of the National Soldiers' Cemetery. [4]As thousands of people gathered there on the bright, sunny day, wood coffins awaiting burial could be seen in the open field.

[5]The first speaker, Edward Everett, spoke for two hours. [6]Lincoln spoke for about two minutes, but his speech had such power that it is considered one of the greatest speeches in history. [7]Here is what he said:

The Gettysburg Address

[8]*"Four score and seven years ago, our fathers brought forth on this continent a new nation, conceived in liberty and dedicated to the proposition that all men are created equal.*

[9]*Now we are engaged in a great civil war, testing whether that nation, or any nation so conceived and so dedicated, can long endure.* [10]*We are met on a great battle field of that war.* [11]*We have come to dedicate a portion of that field, as a final resting place for those who here gave their lives that this nation might live.* [12]*It is altogether fitting and proper that we should do this.*

[13]*But, in a larger sense, we cannot dedicate — we cannot consecrate — we can not hallow this ground.* [14]*The brave men, living and dead, who struggled here, have consecrated it, far above our poor power to add or detract.* [15]*The world will little note, nor long remember, what we say here, but it can never forget what they did here.* [16]*It is for us the living, rather, to be dedicated to the unfinished work which they who fought here have thus far so nobly advanced.* [17]*It is rather for us to be here dedicated to the great task remaining before us — that from these honored dead we take increased devotion to that cause for which they gave the last full measure of devotion — that we here highly resolve that these dead shall not have died in vain — that this nation, under God, shall have a new birth of freedom — and that government of the people, by the people, for the people, shall not perish from the earth."*

Teaching Note: For extra credit, have students memorize and then recite aloud the first sentence of the Gettysburg Address.

Name: ______________________________ **Date:** ________________________________

DIRECTIONS: Identify the best answer for each of the following questions using the evidence presented on the last page. When required, list specific sentence numbers to support your answer.

1. In sentence 8, how many years is "four score and seven years?"

   ____

2. In sentence 9, what does the word *endure* mean?

   A. shake up, bother

   B. to capture or conquer

   C. to continue, to remain firm

   D. to go backwards

3. Was it an easy fight for either side? Which sentence gives the best evidence?

   ____

4. At the dedication, what did the people see that reminded them that thousands of soldiers had died in the battle of Gettysburg?

   ____

   ____

   Give the number of the sentence that best supports your answer. Sentence____

5. Why do you think Lincoln's speech at Gettysburg overshadowed Edward Everett's speech?

   ____

   ____

   Give the number of the sentence that best supports your answer. Sentence____

6. In sentence 8, who was Lincoln talking about when he said "our fathers?"

   ____

   ____

7. Did Lincoln think it was right to dedicate the new cemetery?

   ____

   Give the number of the sentence that best supports your answer.

   Sentence ____

8. Who did Lincoln think had already dedicated the cemetery?

   ____

   Give the number of the sentence that best supports your answer.

   Sentence ____

9. What did Lincoln think people would always remember about Gettysburg?
   A. the dedication of the cemetery
   B. what the speakers said to the crowd
   C. the bravery of the soldiers who fought and died there
   D. the weather the day of the dedication

   Give the number of the sentence that best supports your answer.

   Sentence ____

10. What did Lincoln fear would disappear if the Union lost the war?

    ____

    ____

    Give the number of the sentence that best supports your answer.

    Sentence ____

Note: For more activities like this one, see our *Reading Detective®*, *Math Detective®*, and *Science Detective®* series.

Name: ______________________________ **Date:** ________________________________

Creative Writing

Write a letter: Pretend you are Abraham Lincoln, president of the United States, and you are writing a letter to your former law partner, William "Billy" Herndon, telling him what it is like being president during the Civil War. Use the example of the letter on the next page to write your letter on page 76.

Hints

Introduce the setting: Where are you sitting as you write the letter? Are you in your office, or at a desk in your bedroom? Is it early morning, before you go downstairs to work, or is it late in the evening, before you go to bed?

How do you feel about the war? Are you glad the North and South are fighting? Was it your idea to go to war?

Discuss your home life and how you interact with your family. Is it difficult being the president and a husband and father? Do your children like living in the White House?

Discuss the problems of your job. What are the biggest challenges you're facing? Is it hard being the president? Is it an enjoyable job? Are you happy?

Main events: Think about the main events that will help solve the problems. Give some details about the main events.

Advice: Ask Billy for his advice on how to solve your problems. Tell him you'd appreciate his suggestions.

Example of a Friendly Letter

(Heading)
123 Pine Street
Seattle, WA 98207
January 12, 2009

(Greeting)
Dear Mark,

(Body)

It seems like a long time since I have seen you. I hope you had a nice vacation from school. I spent most of my vacation on the ski slopes.

I hope we can see each other this coming summer. It would be fun to meet at the beach for a couple of days. We could play on the beach and swim in the ocean.

I will ask my parents to call your parents to see if they can plan a vacation together. I think they will think this is a good idea.

Don't you think this would be fun?

(Closing)
Yours truly,
Simon

Name: ______________________ Date: ______________________

Friendly Letter

Name: ______________________________ Date: ______________________________

Research Paper

Write a research paper on one of the other people mentioned in the book.

Some possible people are:

- John Wilkes Booth
- Edward Everett
- Dred Scott
- John C. Fremont
- Andrew Johnson
- Robert E. Lee
- Mary Todd Lincoln
- George Meade
- James Polk
- William T. Sherman
- Any other person mentioned in the index of the book.

The paper should include paragraphs on the following topics:

- Birth, family background, early childhood
- Schooling, adolescent years, young adult years, interests
- Adult years, professions or jobs, reasons or events that made the person famous, contributions made to society, private life
- Later years, death, and how the person is remembered

Some possible resources to use to gather information are:

- Encyclopedias
- Biographies/autobiographies
- Internet
- Trade books
- History books

Name: ______________________ **Date:** ______________________

Research Paper Notes

Gather your information about the person you chose by taking notes in a list form from the different resources you used. Make sure you use at least two different resources. Your notes should contain just the important information you want to use in as few words as possible.

Example: George Meade, born Dec. 31, 1815 (encyclopedia)

Born of American parents in Spain (biography)

Name: ______________________________ **Date:** ________________________________

Now, go back over your notes and label each one. Use a number to show in which paragraph you will use the information. The paragraphs of your paper should include:

1. Introduction
2. Early Childhood
3. Adolescent/Young Adult
4. Adult
5. Senior Years
6. Conclusion

Research Paper 1st Draft

Directions: Use a separate piece of paper to write 6 paragraphs using the instructions below. Do not use I, me, my, myself, our, we, you, your, or any other first or second person pronouns in your first 3 paragraphs.

Title: ____

Paragraph 1: Write an introduction stating who you are writing about.

a. Get your audience interested in reading your paper.
b. Give official title/background of individual/interesting fact about the person.
c. 3 or more sentences

Paragraph 2: Write a topic sentence about the person's childhood.

a. Include information about the person's birth, family background, and early childhood.
b. Include supporting details of interest.
c. 6 or more sentences

Paragraph 3: Adolescent Years

a. Write a topic sentence about the person's adolescent years.
b. Include information about schooling, teenage years, interests, and young adult years.
c. Include supporting details of interest.
d. 6 or more sentences

Paragraph 4: Adult Years

a. Write a topic sentence about the person's adult years.
b. Include information about professions or jobs, reasons or events that made the person famous, contributions to society, and private life.
c. Include supporting details of interest.
d. 6 or more sentences

Paragraph 5: Senior Years

a. Write a topic sentence about the person's later life.

b. Include information about interests in later years, death, and how the person is remembered.

c. Include supporting details of interest.

d. 6 or more sentences

Paragraph 6: Closing Paragraph

a. Bring ideas together, letting the readers know you are concluding your paper.
   - Summarize the main events of the person's life.
   - Draw a conclusion (what you have learned about this person by writing this paper).
   - Give your opinion on the person.

b. 4 or more sentences

Name: ______________________________ **Date:** ______________________________

Research Paper
Editing (CUPS) 1st Draft

Directions: First, make all the necessary changes in red on your first draft by yourself. ***Reread each paragraph 4 times*** checking for the following corrections:

1. *CAPITAL LETTERS*
2. *WORD USAGE*
3. *PUNCTUATION*
4. *SPELLING.*

Next, have a partner give you suggestions and initial each part as you complete it together.

	1st Paragraph Introduction	2nd Paragraph Childhood	3rd Paragraph Adolescent	4th Paragraph Adulthood	5th Paragraph Senior	6th Paragraph Conclusion
"C"apital Letters	You	You	You	You	You	You
	Partner	Partner	Partner	Partner	Partner	Partner
Word "U"sage	You	You	You	You	You	You
	Partner	Partner	Partner	Partner	Partner	Partner
"P"unctuation	You	You	You	You	You	You
	Partner	Partner	Partner	Partner	Partner	Partner
"S"pelling	You	You	You	You	You	You
	Partner	Partner	Partner	Partner	Partner	Partner

Now write your final draft, using the next two pages. Make sure to include your editing changes.

Name: ______________________ Date: ______________________

Final Draft

Name: ______________________ **Date:** ______________________

Name: ______________________________ Date: ________________________________

Research Paper Grade Sheet
Abraham Lincoln and Stephen Douglas

(Put in the grading scale used on progress report card from the school.)

_______ Plans and composes writing

_______ Revises writing

_______ Edits writing

_______ Communicates effectively using written language

_______ Applies spelling strategies to independent work

_______ Creates legible documents using cursive writing

Grading Scale

_______=___________

_______=___________

_______=___________

_______=___________

_______=___________

Use the checklist below to help score the writing project

______ Did not use the pronouns *I, me, my, mine, myself, our, we, you, your*, or any other 1st or 2nd person pronouns in the 1st three paragraphs.

______ Six paragraphs

1st Paragraph: Introductory Paragraph

______ 3 sentences (at least)

Introduced who you were writing about.

______ Got your audience interested in reading your paper.

______ Gave official title/background of individual/interesting fact.

2nd Paragraph: Early Childhood

______ 6 sentences (at least)

______ Topic sentence about early childhood

______ Included information about birth, family background and early childhood.

______ Included supporting details of interest.

3rd Paragraph: Adolescent Years

______ 6 sentences (at least)

______ Topic sentence about adolescent years

______ Included information about schooling, teenage years, interests and young adult years.

______ Included supporting details of interest.

4th Paragraph: Adult Years

______ 6 sentences (at least)

______ Topic sentence about the adult years

______ Included information about professions or jobs, reasons or events that made the person famous, contributions to society and private life.

______ Included supporting details of interest.

5th Paragraph: Senior Years

_____ 6 sentences (at least)

_____ Topic sentence about the person's later life

_____ Included information about interests in later years, death, how the person is remembered.

_____ Included supporting details of interest.

6th Paragraph: Closing Paragraph

_____ 4 sentences (at least)

_____ Brought ideas together to let the readers know you were concluding your paper.

_____ Summarized the main events of the person's life.

_____ Drew a conclusion. (What have you learned about this person by writing this paper?)

_____ Gave your opinion on the person.

Name: ______________________________ **Date:** ______________________________

Study Questions: Use a separate sheet of paper to answer these questions.

1. Describe the different areas where Lincoln grew up. How did his surroundings help shape him into the person he became?

2. Describe Lincoln's actions throughout his life that demonstrated his honesty.

3. What qualities did Lincoln have that made him a good president?

4. Would you have supported the North or the South in the Civil War? List reasons to support your answer.

5. Predict what the United States would be like if the South had won the Civil War.

6. If we hadn't learned the bitter lessons of the Civil War, of states fighting states, what current issues of the day do you think could spark another Civil War?

ANSWERS

Pre-Reading Activity/K-W-L Chart (Pages X-XI)
The wording of the students' answers will vary, but should include the information on what they know about Abraham Lincoln, what they want to find out, and what they learn in each chapter.

Chapter 1

Page 1 A

Word	Part of Speech
a. perish	verb
b. raging	verb
c. conceived	verb
d. communicate	verb
e. democracy	noun
f. liberty	noun
g. proposition	noun
h. documents	noun

Page 2 B

1. equality
2. freedom
3. created
4. die
5. intense
6. plan
7. papers
8. report

Pages 2-3 C
Answers may vary.

1. The ten-sentence speech given by Lincoln is called the Gettysburg Address.
2. (in any order)
   - Lincoln used the speech to stir people of the North.
   - Lincoln urged the North to continue the struggle to save the nation.
3. (in any order)
   - Lincoln kept America from breaking apart during its greatest crisis, the Civil War.
   - He helped put an end to slavery.
4. a. primary
   b. secondary
   c. secondary
   d. primary
   e. secondary
   f. primary

Chapter 2

Page 4 A

Word	Part of Speech
a. brief	adjective
b. recollected	verb
c. restless	adjective
d. crude	adjective
e. swap	verb
f. scarce	adjective

Page 4 B

1. crude
2. swap
3. restless
4. brief
5. scarce
6. recollected

Page 5 C
These characters must be listed. Traits or facts may vary.

1. Thomas Lincoln - farmer, restless, had legal troubles
2. Sarah - first child of Thomas and Nancy, took over household when her mother died, died in childbirth
3. Dennis Hanks - relative of Nancy Lincoln, moved to Little Pigeon with Thomas and Elizabeth Sparrow at 19
4. Sarah Bush Lincoln - loving and fair-minded, raised Abe and Sarah as her own

Pages 6-7 D

1. a. The family moved to a farm at Sinking Spring in Hardin County.
   b. Students need 3 of these answers. The home:
      - was a log cabin.

- had one door that opened and closed on leather hinges.
- had a packed dirt floor.
- had one room.

2. The Lincolns were not considered poor. Students need 2 of these examples.
   - 80-90% of the white population lived in one-room houses.
   - They were well-fed.
   - They were clothed like other families.
3. a. Lincoln's mother died of milk sickness.
   b. The children were sad and lonely. Sarah had to take over the household, cooking, cleaning, sewing and mending.
4. a. Abe was 9 years old when his mother died.
   b. After his wife's death, Thomas went to Elizabethtown.
   c. He brought back a new wife, and the family wasn't lonely anymore.
5. a. Sarah and Abraham found Sarah Bush Johnston to be a loving and fair-minded woman.
   b. She raised the two stepchildren as if they were her own.
6. Students need 3 of these answers. To educate himself, Lincoln:
   - went to school between spring plowing and fall harvesting.
   - worked out arithmetic problems with charcoal on a board.
   - wrote poetry on blank pages of a "sum book."
   - walked long distances to borrow books and read late into the night.
7. Students need 3 of these answers:
   - He and a friend, Allen Gentry, took a cargo of meat, corn, and flour to New Orleans by way of the Ohio and Mississippi rivers.
   - By day, they used long poles to push the boat along with the current.
   - By night, they tied the boat up along the banks of the river
   - They sold their cargo and boat in New Orleans and returned home by steamer.
   - The trip opened Lincoln's eyes to the world beyond Little Pigeon Creek.

Chapter 3

Page 8 A

Across	Down
3. politics	1. dismissed
4. legislature	2. militia
5. campaign	3. plunged
6. debt	4. lawyer

Pages 9-10 B

Sentences will vary.

1. noun	5. noun
2. noun	6. noun
3. noun	7. noun
4. verb	8. verb

Pages 10-11 C

These characters must be listed. Traits or facts may vary.

1. Denton Offutt — a trader, asked Lincoln to manage his store, said Lincoln was the best wrestler in New Salem, closed his store in 1832
2. Jack Armstrong - town's wrestling champion, leader of the Clary Grove Boys, challenged Lincoln to a wrestling match, declared the match a draw
3. John Todd Stuart - young lawyer from Springfield, had served one term in the legislature

4. Mary Owens - from Kentucky, visiting relatives in New Salem, smart, from a good family, Lincoln liked her

Pages 11-12 D

1. Abe was 21 when the family moved again. He was 6 feet 4 inches tall and was muscular and very strong.
2. (in any order)
   - It meant an end to land clearing and wood splitting.
   - He would get to use his head a little.
3. Lincoln was popular with the Clary Grove Boys because of his physical strength, his storytelling abilities, and his honesty.
4. a. Lincoln sought out people to help improve his mind.
   b. The local schoolmaster lent him history books. A local judge encouraged him to start writing contracts and other legal documents.
5. a. There were not many customers.
   b. The store was closed and Lincoln lost his job.
6. Chief Black Hawk's War began.
7. He was disappointed. He had enjoyed the experience. Politics excited him. He looked forward to the chance to run again.
8. a. He borrowed law books and began to study.
   b. He said your own resolution (determination) to succeed was the most important thing.

Chapter 4

Page 13 A

Word	Part of Speech
a. influential	adjective
b. circuits	noun
c. prospered	verb
d. debater	noun
e. eternal	adjective
f. citizens	noun
g. merchant	noun
h. luxury	noun

Page 14 B

1. luxury
2. influential
3. prospered
4. eternal
5. citizens
6. circuits
7. merchant
8. debater

Pages 14-15 C

These characters must be listed. Traits or facts may vary.

1. Ninian and Elizabeth Edwards - one of Springfield's most fashionable couples, Mary Todd's sister
2. Mary Todd — daughter of a wealthy Kentucky merchant and banker — lived with the Edwards family, had brown hair and blues eyes, could be sweet and charming, always had something to say
3. Robert Todd Lincoln — born Aug. 1, 1843, named after Mary's father
4. William H. Herndon — nine years younger than Lincoln, had just received his license to practice law, always called Lincoln Mr. Lincoln

Page 16 D

a.	9	i.	1
b.	12	j.	5
c.	15	k.	6
d.	3	l.	7
e.	16	m.	14
f.	2	n.	8
g.	10	o.	4
h.	13	p.	11

Pages 17-18 E

1. He accepted an offer to become junior partner in John Todd Stuart's law firm in Springfield.
2. Students need 3 of these answers. The city of Springfield:
   - was a frontier town.
   - had a population of 1,500 people.
   - had hogs rooting in the muddy streets.
   - in the summer, was choking with dust.
   - was beset by prairie fires that rained ashes.
3. (in any order)
   - Lincoln was a gifted speaker.
   - He was a quick and bright debater.
4. a. Lincoln was popular with the working men.
   b. He sought friendships with the more well-to-do and influential citizens of Springfield.
5. Students need 3 of these answers. Lincoln and Mary Todd both:
   - were from Kentucky.
   - loved poetry.
   - were interested in politics.
   - were Whigs.
6. Answers will vary but should include: He felt comfortable because:
   - She could be sweet and charming.
   - He didn't have to try to make conversation because she always had something to say.
   - They had many interests in common.
7. (in any order)
   - She was used to luxury and having many servants.
   - She had no training in keeping house, fixing meals, or caring for an infant.
8. (in any order)
   - He was away as many as 3 months or more at a time.
   - Mary did not like being alone.
9. The law office was messy. Papers and documents were heaped on desks and tables. They were stuffed in drawers and crammed into boxes.

Chapter 5

Page 19 A

Word	Part of Speech
a. slavery	noun
b. treaty	noun
c. perplexed	adjective
d. territory	noun
e. opposition	noun
f. congressman	noun
g. conquer	verb
h. plantations	noun

Page 20 B

1. conquer	5. opposition
2. plantations	6. slavery
3. perplexed	7. territory
4. treaty	8. congressman

Pages 20-21 C

These characters must be listed. Traits or facts may vary.

1. President James K. Polk - claimed Mexico started the war in 1846, became a hero to the nation when Mexico signed a peace treaty giving the United States lots of land, did not seek re-election in 1848
2. General Zachary Taylor — a Whig, became a hero during the Mexican War
3. William H. Seward — former governor of New York, strongly opposed slavery

Pages 21-22 D

1. a. Lincoln wanted a change. He wanted new worlds to conquer.
   b. He sought and won election to the U.S. House of Representatives.
2. a. Students' answers will vary but should include:
      - She got little pleasure from her life in Washington, D.C.
      - She didn't like living in a boardinghouse again.
      - She had few friends.
      - She seldom left her room.
   b. She got fed up and moved with her children to her family in Kentucky.
3. - Lincoln said it wasn't true that the Mexicans had fired on Americans on American soil.
   - He said the president and the Democrats got the country into the war to seize Mexican territory for the United States.
4. It received land that became the present states of California, Nevada, and Utah, most of Arizona and New Mexico, and parts of Wyoming and Colorado.
5. Big plantations required large numbers of slaves to raise cotton, tobacco, and other crops.
6. Lincoln expected to be given a rewarding job.
7. Mary had no wish to live in the wilds of the Pacific Northwest.

Chapter 6 Part 1

Page 23 A

Word	Part of Speech
a. cluttered	adjective
b. hardships	noun
c. vain	adjective
d. complex	adjective
e. corporations	noun
f. tyranny	noun
g. journalist	noun
h. profession	noun

Page 24 B

1. profession
2. cluttered
3. journalist
4. complex
5. vain
6. corporations
7. hardships
8. tyranny

Pages 24-26 C

1. a. 6
   b. 2
   c. 1
   d. 4
   e. 7
   f. 5
   g. 3
2. Herndon did the research and bookwork and Lincoln usually appeared in court.
3. Students need 3 of these answers. Hardships Lincoln faced while riding the circuit:
   - Roads were muddy in the winter.
   - In summer, the roads were choked with dust.

- Guests were attacked by fleas and bedbugs
- Tavern food "was hardly fit for the stomach of a horse."

4. a. Lincoln's trademark was his honesty.
   b. He became known as "Honest Abe."
5. (in any order)
   Two tragic events the Lincolns faced from 1849-1851 were:
   - the death of Eddie Lincoln
   - the death of Lincoln's father, Thomas
6. No, nothing could make Mary forget Eddie. Years later, she would still break down and weep at the mention of his name.
7. a. Lincoln gave Thomas the nickname "Tad" or "Taddie."
   b. Thomas had a large head and squirmed like a tadpole.
8. a. The Lincolns did not believe in disciplining their children.
   b. Herndon wanted to grab those "brats" and "wring their necks."

Chapter 6 Part 2

Page 27 A

Word	Part of Speech
a. trigger	verb
b. bill	noun
c. extension	noun
d. compromise	noun
e. injustice	noun
f. issues	noun
g. vast	adjective

Pages 27-28 B

1. vast
2. extension
3. bill
4. trigger
5. compromise
6. issues
7. injustice

Page 28 C

This character must be listed. Traits or facts may vary.

Stephen Douglas — supported the Kansas-Nebraska Act, worked hard to get the Senate to pass the bill, had been the leader of the Young Democrats in the Illinois Legislature, believed slavery should be decided by the people in the territories

Page 29 D

Summaries will vary.

Pages 30-31 E

1. a. the Kansas-Nebraska Act
   b. Settlers in the new territories could decide for themselves whether they wanted slavery.
2. It could have been called the Kansas-Nebraska-North Dakota-South Dakota-Montana-Northern Colorado Act.
3. It allowed the spread of slavery and gave it new life.
4. a. Lincoln was surprised, "thunderstruck and stunned."
   b. He said it was wrong to allow slavery into Kansas and Nebraska and called the new law a "great moral wrong and injustice."
5. Douglas believed that the people in the territories should be able to decide whether to keep slaves. Lincoln felt the extension of slavery was wrong.
6. Northerners were furious. They wanted to limit the spread of slavery. Southerners strongly

supported Douglas and his efforts to extend slavery.

7. The anger that developed on both sides of the issue of slavery helped to bring about conditions that led to the Civil War.

Chapter 7

Page 32 A

Word	Part of Speech
a. inhumane	adjective
b. endure	verb
c. dissolved	verb
d. nomination	noun
e. gloomy	adjective
f. prohibit	verb

Pages 32-33 B

Sentences will vary.

Page 33 C

These characters must be listed. Traits or facts may vary.

1. John C. Fremont - the Republican Party's first presidential candidate, lost the election to Democrat James Buchanan
2. Dredd Scott — had belonged to Dr. John Emerson, an army surgeon — Scott said he should be declared a free man after the doctor took him to Wisconsin and Missouri, claim was rejected by the Supreme Court

Pages 33-34 D

1. a. The Republican party
   b. They believed slavery was evil and opposed its spread into the Western territories.
2. a. The Supreme Court rejected Scott's claim.
   b. Students need 2 of these reasons. The court:
      - declared slaves were not citizens.
      - said slaves could not sue for their freedom.
      - stated Congress had no right to prohibit slavery in any territory.
3. a. Lincoln believed the decision was wrong.
   b. He argued that the Declaration of Independence had declared all men were equal.
4. (in any order)
   - The Republican Party must stop the spread of slavery.
   - They must put slavery back on "the course of ultimate extinction."
5. a. Lincoln felt gloomy.
   b. He was hurt by the defeat.

Page 35 E

Answers will vary, but should include the following:

Lincoln: Republicans' candidate for U.S. Senate, 6 feet 4 inches tall, clothes hung on his lanky frame, believed slavery was wrong and should be restricted to the South.

Both: Ran for U.S. Senate in 1858, participated in a series of debates, were exhausted by the final debate.

Douglas: Democrats' candidate for U.S. Senate, 5 feet 4 inches tall, clothes fitted him neatly, believed Congress should allow people to decide for themselves if slavery was good or evil.

Chapter 8

Page 36 A

Word	Part of Speech
a. secede	verb
b. inauguration	noun
c. severe	adjective
d. launched	verb
e. ambitions	noun
f. oppose	verb

Page 36 B

1. severe
2. secede
3. ambitions
4. inauguration
5. launched
6. oppose

Pages 37-38 C

1. Lincoln's name began to be mentioned as a possible candidate for the presidential election of 1860.
2. Lincoln admitted that he liked the idea of running for president.
3. He said Republicans shouldn't be afraid to oppose slavery; that it was the right thing to do. He noted that being right would give them the power to help achieve their goals.
4. a. Before the election, Southern leaders had urged Southern states to secede from the Union if Lincoln won.
   b. Lincoln thought the people of the South "had too much good sense and good temper" to secede.
   c. No, he was wrong.
5. a. The first state to leave the Union was South Carolina.
   b. The next five states to leave were Alabama, Mississippi, Georgia, Florida, and Louisiana.

Chapter 9

Page 39 A

Across	Down
1. wounded	2. occasionally
3. ports	4. surrender
5. crisis	6. fleet
7. industrial	
8. urgent	

Pages 40-41B

Sentences will vary.

1. adjective
2. noun
3. noun
4. noun
5. adjective
6. noun
7. adverb
8. verb

Page 41 C

a. 8	h. 10
b. 7	i. 4
c. 13	j. 11
d. 5	k. 6
e. 1	l. 12
f. 9	m. 2
g. 3	

Page 42 D

These characters must be listed. Traits or facts may vary.

1. General Robert Anderson — wrote to Lincoln, saying his supplies would be gone in six weeks; refused when the Confederates demanded surrender; was forced to give up after a heavy pounding
2. General Robert E. Lee - commanded Confederate forces at the battle for Richmond, was a brilliant leader

Pages 42-44 E

1. He had to decide whether to hold on to Fort Sumter or order General Robert Anderson to abandon it.
2. • It could trigger a civil war.
   • If he gave up Sumter, he would be considered weak.
3. • Lincoln could not make up his mind.
   • A week went by, then two weeks; then a month.
   • Northern newspapers called on Lincoln to do something.
4. He ordered Navy ships to take supplies to Fort Sumter. When the Confederates learned the ships were on the way they demanded surrender and then opened fire.
5. The North because:
   • It had more people.
   • It had greater industrial strength.
6. a. Many Northerners believed a major battle would end the war and pressured Lincoln to act.
   b. The Northerners were shocked and gave up their belief that the war would end quickly.
7. Students need 3 of these answers. It was evident that Tad and Willie ran wild at the White House because:
   • They burst into office meetings.
   • They played tricks on the White House staff.
   • They collected more than a dozen pets.
   • They rode a pony around the White House grounds.
   • A goat slept in Tad's bed.
   • They held executions of dolls.
8. After two years of war, Lincoln seemed to grow stronger and more determined. He believed that the Union must be saved. He meant to achieve that goal no matter the cost.

Chapter 10

Page 45 A

Word	Part of Speech
a. amendment	noun
b. ratified	verb
c. emancipate	verb
d. rebellion	noun
e. symbol	noun
f. outlawed	verb

Page 46 B

1. rebellion
2. emancipate
3. symbol
4. amendment
5. ratified
6. outlawed

Pages 46-48 C

1. Lincoln was a patient man. Students need 2 of these answers.
   • He could put up with long delays.
   • He could wait for the right moment.
   • Lincoln believed it was better to let events unfold naturally.
2. a. Lincoln felt it was best to let slavery alone in the South.
   b. He believed that once the war was won, slavery would gradually die out.
3. a. He believed the war was being waged to restore the Union.
   b. They said slavery was the main cause of the war.
4. (in any order)
   a. Delaware, Kentucky, Maryland, and Missouri
   b. They were called the border states.

c. All those states allowed slavery.

5. The border states would be angered and might join the Confederacy.
6. It was symbolic, it offered hope to enslaved people that they would be freed once the Union won the war.
7. No, it could not be enforced in the rebel states and did not apply to border states.
8. a. Lincoln realized the Emancipation Proclamation did not do enough to free the slaves.

   b. The Thirteenth Amendment outlawed slavery in every part of America forever.

Chapter 11

Page 49 A

Word	Part of Speech
a. politely	adverb
b. equality	noun
c. deserted	verb
d. climax	noun
e. draft	verb
f. policies	noun
g. discontent	noun
h. unrest	noun

Page 50 B

1. draft
2. unrest
3. deserted
4. politely
5. climax
6. policies
7. equality
8. discontent

Pages 50-51 C

These characters must be listed. Traits or facts may vary.

1. General Joseph Hooker - commanded the Union army of some 100,000 men, said the Confederates outnumbered him, wanted more troops, was believed by Lincoln to be afraid to fight
2. General George Meade - He was sour-faced and bad-tempered. Troops called him "a goggle-eyed old snapping turtle." His Union victory was the turning point of the war.
3. Edward Everett - one of the greatest speakers of the day, spoke first, spoke for two hours

Pages 51-52 D

1. No. He was deeply troubled.
   - His generals kept disappointing him.
   - He wanted a general who would fight harder.
2. a. Many were killed on the battlefield. Thousands of others had deserted their units.

   b. The government decided to draft young men into the army.
3. a. The Southerners were strongly opposed to the idea.

   b. They were afraid the slaves would turn on their masters.
4. a. Angry Northerners protested the draft and spoke out against the Emancipation Proclamation.

   b. Lincoln made it clear both would continue to be the law of the land.
5. Students need 3 of these answers.
   - Lee sent 15,000 men toward the center of the Union lines.
   - Union soldiers watched as the Southerners advanced in orderly lines.
   - Union artillery began pounding away.
   - Union riflemen hit the Southerners with murderous fire.
   - The beaten Confederates fell back.

- Half of the original force lay dead or wounded.
- Lee ordered a full retreat.

6. (in any order)
   - It was the turning point in the war.
   - Lee's crippled army would never again launch a major attack.
7. Lincoln was referring to 1776 and the Declaration of Independence.
8. Students need 2 of these answers.
   - The audience applauded politely.
   - He remarked to a friend "it fell upon the audience like a wet blanket."
   - Most newspapers gave much more space to Everett's speech.

Chapter 12

Page 53 A

Word	Part of Speech
a. desperate	adjective
b. malice	noun
c. battered	adjective
d. charity	noun
e. tactics	noun
f. strive	verb
g. oath	noun

Page 53 B

1. lie
2. guesswork
3. rebuilt
4. confident
5. kindness
6. hatred
7. quit

Page 54 C

These characters must be listed. Traits or facts may vary.

1. General Ulysses S. Grant - 42, born in Port Pleasant, Ohio; skilled horseman at West Point; served as a captain in the Mexican War; left the army in 1854; signed up again in 1861, when Lincoln called for volunteers
2. George B. McClellan - failed Lincoln as commander of the Union army, promised to bring peace "at the earliest possible moment," said he would restore the Union and permit slavery, lost to Lincoln by almost a half-million votes

Pages 54-56 D

1. They would attack on all fronts and would launch "total war."
2. - Grant led an attack on Lee's troops in Virginia.
   - Sherman's army advanced through Tennessee and Georgia toward Atlanta.
3. (in any order)
   - He believed he was the best person to keep the Union together.
   - It would serve as a stamp of approval.
4. (in any order)
   - McClellan had promised to bring peace "at the earliest possible moment."
   - Support for the war was fading.
5. (in any order)
   - The Northerners felt more confident about Lincoln.
   - Lincoln defeated McClellan by almost a half-million votes.
6. (in any order)
   - It was not long.
   - It did not waste words.
   - It was forceful and moving.
7. Students need 2 of these answers.
   - There was a shortage of food and supplies.
   - There was a terrible loss of life.

- There was widespread sadness and gloom.

8. a. He was curious to see the now-battered city, which had become the symbol of the Confederacy.
   b. Students need 3 of these answers.
      - They saw some buildings that were still burning.
      - Thick, black smoke hung over the city.
      - Crowds of cheering, laughing, freed slaves gathered around.
      - Hundreds of people flocked around Lincoln.

Chapter 13

Page 57 A

Word	Part of Speech
a. threatening	adjective
b. routine	adjective
c. engaged	verb
d. heartily	adverb
e. saluted	verb
f. convicted	verb
g. parlor	noun
h. unconscious	adjective

Page 58 B

1. threatening
2. unconscious
3. routine
4. heartily
5. saluted
6. parlor
7. convicted
8. engaged

Page 58 C

These characters must be listed. Traits or facts may vary.

1. Henry R. Rathbone - young army major, engaged to Clara Harris, lunged at the gunman who shot Lincoln, his arm was cut in the struggle
   - Clara Harris - engaged to Henry R. Rathbone, screamed that the president had been shot and for someone to stop Booth
2. John Wilkes Booth - noted actor of the day, supported the Confederacy, approved of slavery, believed Lincoln was responsible for the war, broke a bone in his leg leaping from the president's box but got away, was eventually hunted down by Union soldiers, shot and killed in a tobacco barn near Port Royal, Virginia.

Page 58-60 D

1. General Lee had surrendered.
2. a. He was overjoyed.
   b. The president and Stanton threw their arms around each other.
3. a. They wanted to punish the Confederate leaders.
   b. No, Lincoln took a softer approach. He wanted to help rebuild and restore the South. He wanted to protect the rights of the freed slaves.
4. They feared that someone who had supported the Confederate cause would kidnap or kill him.
5. Students need 5 of these answers.
   - A man came into the president's box.
   - He shot the president in the head.
   - Mary threw her arms around her husband and screamed.
   - Major Rathbone lunged at the gunman.
   - The attacker leaped from the box to the stage.
   - When he fell to the stage, he broke his leg.
   - Limping across the stage, he shouted, *"Sic semper tyrannis!"* (Thus it shall ever be for tyrants.)

- The attacker went to an alley at the back of the stage.
- He got on a horse and galloped away.

6. The president died in the bedroom of a narrow, 3-story house across the street from the theater.
7. a. At each stop, mourners were given a chance to file past Lincoln's open coffin. There was an overpowering feeling of loss.
   b. Springfield, Illinois

Chapter 14

Page 61A

Word	Part of Speech
a. indicate	verb
b. erected	verb
c. accounts	noun
d. awesome	adjective
e. towering	adjective
f. complaints	noun
g. minted	verb
h. mourning	noun

Page 62 B

1. towering
2. mourning
3. minted
4. accounts
5. awesome
6. erected
7. complaints
8. indicate

Pages 62-63C

1. Answers will vary but students should have three of the following:
   - People felt shock, then grief.
   - Houses, shops, and buildings were decorated with black ribbon and other signs of mourning.
   - People hung memorial portraits of Lincoln in their homes.
   - People pinned on mourning ribbons.
   - Some wore pins or badges bearing Lincoln's portrait.
2. a. They thought Lincoln should have been honored with a more important coin.
   b. Others argued the penny was proper since Lincoln was "the people's president."
3. Answers will vary, but students should have three of the following:
   - the five-dollar bill
   - the one hundred-dollar bill
   - postage stamps
   - medals
   - tokens
4. Lincoln's name represents honesty.

Page 64 Events/Sequence

Year	Order
1809	1st
1861	10th
1836	4th
1860	8th
1865	16th
1864	13th
1858	7th
1842	5th
1863	12th
1834	3rd
1865	15th
1863	11th
1865	14th
1846	6th
1832	2nd
1861	9th

Pages 65-70 Compare/Contrast
Students write a compare/contrast paper about Lincoln and Douglas using the worksheets provided.

Pages 71-73 Reading Detective®

1. 87
2. C. to continue, to remain firm
3. The battle was difficult for both sides. Sentence 2: "The fighting was fierce and both sides suffered many deaths and injuries."
4. They saw wood coffins awaiting burial in the open field. Sentence 4
5. Everett spoke for more than two hours, while Lincoln only spoke for about 2 minutes but his words were powerful. Sentence 6
6. Lincoln was referring to the founding fathers and the American Revolution.
7. Yes, Lincoln thought it was "fitting and proper" to do so. Sentence 12
8. The soldiers in the battle of Gettysburg had already dedicated the cemetery. Sentence 14
9. C. the bravery of the soldiers who fought and died there. Sentence 15
10. the nation, the United States of America and its government. Sentence 17

Pages 74-76 Creative Writing
Students write a letter as Lincoln to a former law partner about his job as president during the Civil War.

Pages 77-85 Research Paper
Students write a research paper on one of the other people mentioned in the book using the worksheets.

Pages 86-87 Book Study Questions
Answers may vary. Some possible answers are listed.

1. Lincoln's family lived on land in Kentucky, Indiana, and Illinois, which he helped turn into farms with his father. The hard work made him physically and mentally strong. His father sometimes had legal problems with his land dealings, which could have sparked Lincoln's interest in the law. While he was growing up, he often helped people, leading to a life of public service.

2. A book he borrowed from a neighbor got soaked. He worked on the neighbor's farm to repay the cost of the ruined book. He always told the truth. When the country store he and a partner bought failed, he worked odd jobs, including as a farmhand, for years, to pay off the debt. He became known as "Honest Abe," because of his absolute honesty. He advised those considering going into the law that if they couldn't be honest lawyers, they should seek other careers.

3. He was patient; he waited before acting during the Civil War. He was patriotic; he served his country through the militia and as a political leader. He was absolutely honest. His goal as a political leader was to keep the country together. He was determined; even after losing political battles, he continued to run for public office. Despite the terrible presssures of the war and the presidency, he pressed on, even running for a second term.

4. Answers will vary.

5. Answers will vary.

6. Answers will vary.